Love E Guide To Style

Evonya Easley

Illustrated by: Erin McManness

Copyright © 2014 by: Evonya Easley

All rights reserved. Except as permitted under the U.S Copyright Act of 1976, no part of this publication may be reproduced, distributed, or transmitted in any form or by any means, or stored in a database or retrieval system, without the prior written permission of the author, except for the inclusion of brief quotations in a review.

Soft Cover Edition

ISBN: 978-0-9899280-1-4

First Edition 2014.

Printed in the United States of America.

Love E Guide to Style

Written by: Evonya Easley
Produced by: LoriganRespres, A New Day Publishing
Illustrated by: Erin McManness

Published by: A New Day Publishing www.anewdaybooks.com

Thank you to my sweetie Anthony Kirkland for all his support an always having my back to pursue all my dreams and helping them become my reality.

Thank you to my daughter Lynelle Joy, and everyone else in my family that has supported me in this endeavor.

This book is dedicated to all of my clients who allowed me to come in and enhance their wardrobe, which in turn has enriched their lives!

INTRO

"I dress for the image. Not for myself, not for the public, not for fashion, not for men."

MARLENE DIETRICH

Intro: *This book is for all the women who want to be a fashionista; but do not have the time to do so. Here are some quick tips that explain what is needed in your wardrobe, as well as how to put it together. This book is a down to earth - relaxed guide about developing personal style for up and coming fashionistas, or people who want to present their best to the world.*

It will give you a guide for what you should have in your closet, such as the basics; how to build upon those basics, what to buy, how to shop and how to put everything together to make a more fabulous you. I will be taking you into a visual tour of my own closet and showing you how over time I was able to build up an impressive wardrobe over the years. I never have to repeat myself. I just keep reinventing.

As my style evolves, so does my closet. I do an inventory every season and get rid of items that are no longer working for me. I may toss something because I can no longer fit it or I maybe I feel that it is no longer a representation of my personality. Next, I take a look at what the trends are for the season and decide which pieces actual apply and work for me.

I try to pick up pieces that will work can be easily coordinated with what I already have. And that ladies, is how over time you can have everything you need in your closet right at your fingertips to become a well-dressed woman. You will now be ready and armed for every occasion that may come your way.

alexander mcqueen

"It's a new era in fashion-- there are no rules. It's all about the individual and personal style, wearing high-end, low-end, classic labels, and up-and-coming designers all together."

FASHION FADES

Style is Eternal

"Style" is an expression of individualism mixed with charisma. Fashion is something that comes after style."

- john fairchild

"Style is a way to say who you are without having to speak."

- rachel zoe

"Be sure of what you want and be sure about yourself. Fashion is not just beauty, it's about good attitude. You have to believe in yourself and be strong."

- adriana lima

First things first, let's discuss why you should care about your appearance. This world is a visual world; where everything around us from ads, commercials, TV, and people make judgments based on what they see, regardless of whether those opinions are right or not. First impressions and how you carry yourself are everything and what you wear will affect and in some cases determine how people perceive you.

When I help my clients, I'm always thinking that you never know what could happen when they are wearing an ensemble I put together for them. They may get that dream job from the outfit I put together, that they wore to the interview or they could meet their significant other on the day they are wearing a look I put together.

Anything could happen, and I am proud that I may have played a small role in assisting with that. It makes me happy to enrich someone's life in small way, by just giving them a wardrobe that helps them be perceived the way they want to be perceived.

> "While clothes may not make the woman, they certainly have a strong effect on her self-confidence — which,
> I believe, does make the woman."
> — Mary Kay Ashe

To me, style is like makeup. One shouldn't put on so much makeup that they are unrecognizable. Makeup should enhance a person's natural beauty. With style, the same concept applies. I prefer not to put clients in clothes that make them uncomfortable or clothes that do not complement their lifestyle. I just want to enhance people's personal style and upgrade it a bit.

If necessary, I also love to teach them how to shop and dress and how to build on the foundation of clothes they already have. I also want to help them find their personal style, whatever that may be so they can stick to it. Whether their style is very relaxed, bohemian, chic or classic or a siren,

I want to make my clients feel their best and look good. When well dressed, you have a tendency to feel good and have a strut in your walk and pep in your step.

"I HAVE ALWAYS BELIEVED THAT FASHION WAS NOT ONLY TO MAKE WOMEN MORE BEAUTIFUL, BUT ALSO TO REASSURE THEM, GIVE THEM CONFIDENCE."

– Yves Saint Laurent

"Don't be into trends. Don't make fashion own you, but you decide what you are, what you want to ex- press by the way you dress and the way you live."
— Gianni Versace

THE BASICS

"Only great minds can afford a simple style"

— STENDHAL

The Basics

The basic concept of building a wardrobe is the idea of starting from the foundation of what you have and building upon that and moving forward. First of all, all women need to identify their personal style and know that style is different from fashion. Fashion is about the trends, colors and most elements of fashion come go and eventually circles back around.

Style is about wearing what works for you, your personality, life and body. My personal style is always going to be classic but sexy and with an edge. I love the shape of a woman and her silhouette, so I always dress with that in mind and prefer to always have some shape to my clothes. I then take that particular style and dress everyday based on my mood, the weather and what shoes I want to wear that day.

With my clients, I try find out their personal style first before moving forward with shaping their wardrobe. I try to find out if they are a tomboy, classic, conservative, edgy etc. And from there, I build their wardrobe according to how they would like to look - starting in their closet first. Once we have figured out their personal style, what they should always wear, what looks good on them and what they feel good in - the trends become less important.

If miniskirts are in, but pencil skirts look better on a particular client, then they should wear pencil skirts. Everything about fashion comes in style goes out and comes back in again like the circle of life, but it's the circle of style.

Once the client's style is narrowed down, we start working on their closet so that I can purge clothing that does not fit them properly. Anything that does not fit or flatter your body must go! Next, we look to see what does work in your closet so that we can build on that and go from there.

Prime example: If you have great bottoms, but barely any tops, we would look for more tops to go with your bottoms. We would add accessories and always add more shoes!! I don't believe there is a such thing as too many shoes! We will talk more about that in another section of the book.

Again, one of the first steps in working in the closet is editing what works for you. You have to ask yourself; how do you want to be
perceived? Do you want to be viewed as Hollywood like Audrey Hepburn or a siren like a Marilyn Monroe or perhaps edgy like Rihanna?

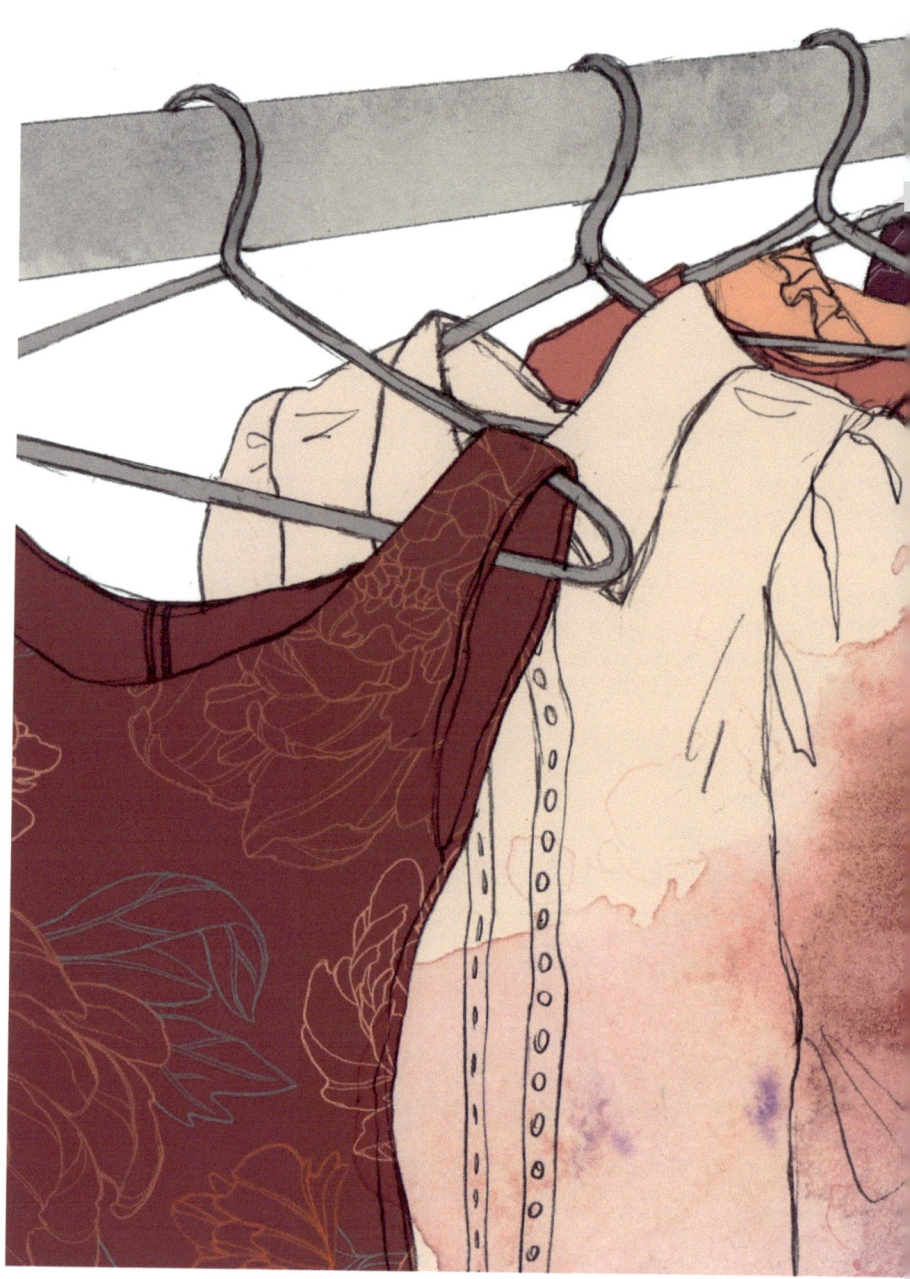

"One is never over-dressed or underdressed with a Little Black Dress."
— Karl Lagerfeld

The next principle to follow is that you need to have some basic pieces in your closet: This includes a LBD (Little Black Dress), trench coat, black heels, a quality tee and a nice handbag. A crisp white shirt, a pair of flats, pencil skirt, a blazer, a few simple and dramatic accessories are a must!

Also, try not to be tempted to just buy things on sale just because it's on sale. If it does not work for you, do not buy it period! Buying the proper size clothing is important and looking good in every size as you lose or gain weight is important as well. Don't forget to have fun with your wardrobe. It should not be all trendy and shouldn't be all conservative either. Invest money in the classics and basic necessities and have an occasional trendy piece in as an accent.

little black dress

CLASSICS

"It is the unseen, unforgettable, ultimate accessory of fashion that heralds your arrival and prolongs your departure.

- COCO CHANEL

ACCESSORIES

"I think the accessories look very modern and very exciting. These big earrings, these big hoops. I think the girls are sort of falling in love with... collars, neck collars."

— RALPH LAUREN

Accessories can add to every outfit, even if it's as simple as a tank and jeans. Pairing that with some hoops and lots of bangles going up your arm will make that simple ensemble look great.

Your accessories should include a great watch, nice earrings, bracelets and bangles as well as great rings. You also need funky or cocktail statement pieces (also known as costume jewelry to add to your look and make it complete.

WHAT DO Women Want?

Shoes

—mimi pond

SHOES

Give a girl the right shoes and she can conquer the world.

— MARILYN MONROE

> "I never wear flats. My shoes are so high that sometimes when I step out of them, people look around in confusion and ask, "Where'd she go?" and I have to say, "I'm down here."
>
> -Marian Keyes

I have eight pairs of black shoes; however black is my least favorite color when it comes to dressing because I love color. Black is a foundation color a basic color and so are colors like brown, and cream/white. So now, I d like to share the details and explain my 8 pair of black shoes for you because again, there is a method to my madness. For starters, I have my summer black and my winter black. My winter black consists of a pair of flat black boots for those days where you know I am going to be on my feet all day and just can't bear wearing a pair of stilettos.

I must admit that I have those days every now and then, though I am not a fan of flat shoes at all. My flats have to be extraordinary to make up for the fact they are flats. Of course I am not judging anyones preference, this is just my viewpoint and I understand that some people can only or desire only to wear flats. As always, everyone has to do what is best for them.

So continuing on with my explanation about my various pairs of black shoes: I have my black flat winter boots, I have my black lace up dominatrix style boots that come up over my knees, which is a very sexy boot. Everybody doesn't have a need for a sexy boot but I do. This style of boot is perfect for a cold night out.

The boot covers most of your leg so you instantly have additional warmth without having to give up your personal style for those unpredictable winter evenings. There is also the option to have a black knee high boot with a heel. - Whether it be a wedge or skinny heel, this style of boot is a perfect daytime boot to wear with some skinny jeans and great coat.

Next, I have a pair of booties that stop at the ankle. I also have a pair of closed toe boots as well as a pair of peekaboo male-inspired shoes that gives a masculine edge to a totally feminine look. These can be worn with tights and a dress or with a flirty skirt. This approach just adds a touch of funk to an otherwise girly look. I have one closed toe boot and an open toe version as well because a girl needs options.

The closed toe boot is definitely for when I do not want any toe cleavage exposed, either because I need a pedicure or because it is cold. The open toe boot can work for me year round, which is what I love about open toe shoes. They give enough coverage for the Fall/Winter but also have enough of your foot left out for the Spring/Summer. That is definitely a year-round shoe. You never have to worry about being over exposed like with a sandal or underexposed like a "Normal" boot.

Now my summer version of the basic black shoe is pretty simple. I have a daytime black sandal and a sexy/edgy, nighttime pair of black sandals. Sometimes these shoes can be one in the same but most times this is not the case. A black wedge type shoe is most likely a daytime look. Additionally, everyone needs a black flat for those days in the summer where you do not want to wear a heel and need the color black.

I like to be prepared for everything, and I have been working in fashion for a while – so being organized by the beginning of each season. I always make sure that I do a closet inventory to determine what I need/want for the season and then I begin a plan to buy one item a week/bi-weekly/monthly until my list of fashion needs is covered for the season.

The basic shoes that are needed in every wardrobe include: black pumps, black boots, nude pumps, nude boots. One shoe with a pop of color and a pair with some sort of print.. Also, try to go beyond that and try colors like red, cream, white, blue, green, and every color under the rainbow. If you do this, eventually you will have a great collection of shoes and something to go with everything you own as well as future outfits. The same rule goes for accessories. Once you get past the basic accessories, don't be afraid to explore and buy pieces that move you and catch your eye.

Remember that you can use the more flashy pieces for accent pieces to make your look pop. I also make it a point to replace anything that has been worn out in my closet. If a heel needs to be replaced, I go to my local shoe cobbler and let him take care of my precious shoes. If a shoe can be saved, I will try to save it before I discard it.

Once I finally get tired of a particular shoe, I often give it away to a charity. The only way I will throw a shoe in the trash is if it is beyond repair, which is rare in my case. The more shoes you have, the harder it is to wear a specific pair out.

You will always have options to choose from if you keep several pair of shoes, so they all can be well maintained
I have a leopard print pair of shoes with crystals by Betsy Johnson that I saw and just fell in love with. I just had to buy those. If a pair of shoes stands out or catches my eye, I buy them. I have different shades of pink, purple, etc.

"Sometimes comfort doesn't matter. When a shoe is freakin' fabulous, it may be worth a subsequent day of misery. Soak in Epsom salts and take comfort in the fact that you're better than everyone else." Clinton Kelly

I have a tendency to go darker for winter like deep purples, and deep greens. For summer I go with the lavenders, yellows, orange, coral etc. I have some colors that I wear both in the winter summer time. Purple and turquoise are examples of colors that I have both for seasons. I own a purple Mary Jane pump as well as a peep toe summer sandal pump. I have a turquoise suede pump for the winter and a turquoise color block peep toe for the summer. I am a fan of having every color and having a winter and summer version of it, but thats me. So remember to branch out and buy a nude pump or blush colored, bold red, or crystal embedded sandal just because you can.

You will always eventually find an outfit that can complement your shoes. Wearing interesting shoes is also a way to be more daring or venture outside your comfort zone than you do with your wardrobe. Shoes are a small way of making a big statement if you so choose this route.

Plus, shoes are a much safer way to take a risk for the most part. The weight in your feet won't fluctuate the way your body weight will. Shoes are a little more trustworthy, while clothes will betray you within a pound or a few. So I'm more likely to splurge on something that I know I can wear, whether I'm a size 6 or a size 12.

I have this one pair of white fur boots that I can't wear just any ole place or time. I have had them for years. They are beautiful and I wear them once or twice a year, if that. I usually wear them sometime between Christmas and Valentine's Day. They were expensive, but they were a gift so since I have had them so long and wear them so rarely, they are well maintained and now are well worth their cost. I always justify the price of an item by dividing the cost of it by how many years I have a chance to wear it.

If I have the piece a long time, it really wasn't that expensive if I think about how many years it has been in my possession. Hey, don't judge me because this is my logic and my math and as the saying goes: if the shoe works, then wear it! I have so many pairs of black shoes because that is a primary color that a lot of people tend to wear regularly Back to my white boots, those are for special occasion.

It is very rare that I need to wear a white boot outside of this is particular pair, so I only have one pair of white boots. I don't need a bootie or a knee boot in white, not for my lifestyle or for my clothing options. You on the other, hand may wear white all the time and need to wear another color as frequently as I wear black. In brown, I have flat winter brown boots, stiletto boots, and 3 pair of brown pumps. Each look is totally different from each other; one is a sling back with a pattern and a shiny toecap. The other pair has different shades of brown texture, all quilted together. The last pair is brown based, with shades of olive and orange shades throughout. So again, you have to build according to your own personal lifestyle.

I only have the boots and a peep toe stilettos in white. You have to determine what colors you need more and less of. I have a lot of peep toes or pumps in purple, turquoise, olive, pink, fuchsia, and every other color in the rainbow. And now that I have built a solid fashion foundation, I buy what moves me. Whether its multi-color or has textured or has a crazy print or shape, or anything that stands out, I'm likely to buy it.

"I like Cinderella, I really do. She has a good work ethic. I appreciate a good, hard-working gal. And she likes shoes. The fairy tale is all about the shoe at the end, and I'm a big shoe girl." *-Amy Adams*

- bertolt brecht

> "I'm definitely the kind of person to wear underwear all the time."
> —Ashley Tisdale

It is also important to note that control wear can help smooth everything out as well as hold everything in under your clothing. You can get everything from control thongs, waist minimizers and control boy shorts for when you wearing a short dress etc.

No matter which brand you are looking for, you can find control wear just about anywhere - from Target to Nordstroms and boutiques as well;,

I suggest trying whichever brand is in your budget and works best for your body. I do not want to recommend any particular brand because not every brand is for everybody. Once you have the proper undergarments, it's time for the clothes yea!!

UNDERGARMENTS

"I don't always wear underwear. When I'm in the heat, especially, I can't wear it. Like, if I'm wearing a flower dress, why do I have to wear underwear?"

– NAOMI CAMPBELL

"Dress shabbily and they remember the dress; dress impeccably and they remember the Woman."
— Coco Chanel

It's great to be a woman! Women have so many options and articles of clothing that they can wear as opposed to men. We have dresses, skirts and shorts to name a few, with long or short options for each of these categories. We have tops that range from dressy to casual as well.

Always wear a dress that flatters your shape. One of the most universal dresses that will work for majority of womens body types is the classic wrap dress. Wrap dresses give you a waistline and a shape, regardless of what size you are.

Also, dresses can be can be a great option if you are trying to look more feminine and may work with whatever your personal style and body type is.

Mixing colors are great approach. I personally love the use of color while wearing dresses. Even if you love wearing black; please don't forget to occasionally add a pop of color in your shoes, accessories, a scarf, handbag, or something. A lot of people don't realize all of the different color combinations that can be put together; like chocolate with turquoise, and purple.

Basically, most simple and neutral colors can easily be complimented when adding a pop of color with them. White, black, cream, and brown are all basic colors that can be enhanced with pops of color like red, purple, yellow etc. Theres no excuse not to add a bit of color to almost any and every outfit.

DRESSES

Over the years, I have learned that what is important in a dress is the woman who is wearing it.

— YVES SAINT-LAURENT

One important part of building a wardrobe, especially if you have to do it over time, is to start with your basics and add any and all the colors later. Just one new item a week is 52 pieces by the end of a year, and if you just add something every other week, you get half of that. So you can easily build a nice wardrobe over time. Make sure majority of your purchases are interchangeable with items you already have, as well as future purchases.

If you purchase your basic color bottoms in colors like brown, crème, black, white, or denim, all you need are skirts in those colors, all made in different styles like long, pencil, short or detailed.

Try to focus on wearing all your different tops with all the different bottoms you have, which will basically make all of your pieces interchangeable and will give you more ensembles to wear. You can add to the fun by switching up your accessories as well.

I try to never wear the same combo twice, and at this point I don't have to because I have built up a wardrobe over the years. There is definitely an art to dressing nice without looking like you are trying, and It is a bonus when you effortlessly look nice enough for other people to realize that you care about your appearance.

"I want everyone to wear what they want and mix it in their own way. That, to me, is what is modern." - Karl Lagerfeld

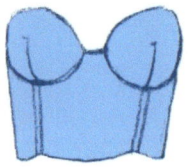

I wore a printed bottom with white, orange and blue in it. Every time I wear those pants I'll wear a different top. I may wear an orange top with orange heels to bring out that color in the pants. Next time, I wear it with a white or blue tank still with the orange heels or a white wedge, just to give it a different look.

I can switch up the heels with the same colors in the pants so by the time I do all the different combos; I have worn that one pair of pants 6/7 different ways. I change up the accessories as I change the look and maybe add a blazer or a crop jacket.

And that principle can be applied to all clothes. If I wear an all-white suit skirt or pant set I can wear any color top underneath every time I wear that suit as well as do an all-white if I want.

Every separate piece of clothing that I own is something that I can wear a minimum 3 different ways, if not more. Dresses are an entire outfit unto themselves. I switch up the shoes, handbags and accessories and add scarfs, blazers, jackets or cropped jackets whenever I want to add a bit of zing to any dress. I may even add a little sweater in order to keep changing a look of a dress.

You can also choose to wear different belts with dresses that require a belt because it is easy to change the appearance of a dress just by switching up belts. For example, I have a dark blue pleated skirt dress that came with a camel belt. I wear it with camel fishnets and my camel boots.

The next time I wore that very same dark blue pleated skirt dress, I wore it with my chocolate belt and boots and switched out my accessories. Adding details to ensembles make them pop, just like adding textured as well as color or printed tights to dresses and skirts make them pop in the winter.

Adding gloves and scarfs to an outfit also adds a little something. It is that extra step that can make you look stylish

JEANS

"I like being a woman, even in a man's world. After all, men can't wear dresses, but we can wear the pants."

— WHITNEY HOUSTON

I'm a mom, so I have to be comfortable. Jeans are a staple - I have way too many in my closet! It's warm in Florida, so I wear jeans and a tank top every day. I love my True Religions, my Rich and Skinny, and Citizens of Humanity. But I also love getting dressed up!

-Candace Cameron Bure

Jeans are one of the items I feel women have too many of. Its only seven days in a week you are not going to wear jeans every day. You don't need twenty pairs of jeans unless you are a collector or some sort. People have too many black pants as well. I say this cause it starts to look like you wearing the same bottoms every day.

A woman needs a dark skinny jean and dark trouser jean. Dark jeans look dressier as if you are wearing trousers instead of jeans. A light colored pair, a printed pair and a fun pair with rips or bleach maybe are the ones you keep to throw on to work in the yard or garden.

If you have a bunch of different jeans they do not need to look all alike. They need to be all slightly different so it doesn't look like the same bottom over and over. The same for black bottoms and black everything. Add some color to your black and also wear grey as an alternative to your black. Everything you can wear with black you can wear with grey. Grey is like the lighter version of black.

I have often said that I wish I had invented blue jeans.

the most spectacular, the most practical, the most relaxed & non-chalant. They have expression, modesty, sex appeal, simplicity—all I hope for in my clothes.

— ysl

Nothing is cute enough to buy it in every color. Buy a different style and different color so it will never look like you are wearing the same thing that you wore another day. Buy more than just plain tees. Buy tops with shape and silhouette and detail.

I call them stand alone pieces so you can wear these tops with just a pair of jeans or pants, cute shoes accessories and go. If everything you own is basic and nondescript it will look monotonous and boring like you are wearing a uniform just with different colors.

You want to get tops in every color again building on what you have and will buy in the future even if you don't have a bottom to go with it yet. Lets say a coral top with white pants, shorts or skirt every color that is not a basic color will go with a basic as reference back to an earlier rule. Coral will go with white, cream, black, blue jean even a print if coral is in that print

"Fashion is very important. It is life-enhancing and, like everything that gives pleasure, it is worth doing well."
Vivienne Westwood

COATS

"I have always believed that fashion was not only to make women more beautiful, but also to reassure them, give them confidence."

- YVES SAINT-LAURENT

Not only should you buy different color tops, but you should also try different fabrics as well such as silks, jersey, soft cotton, structured, stretchy lace, leather, etc. You should also try different shapes of tops like a wrap around, sleeveless, ruffles, peplum, 3 quarter, bell sleeve, pleats, draping, back out, button down, high-low tops and the list goes on and on.

This way you will have a variety of styles to choose from to go with your skirts, shorts, jeans, trousers and any other bottoms you may have. Colored bottoms sometimes tend to look like a trend or a fad or too youthful, so be careful with buying a pair of fuchsia pants versus a top; the top will last much longer than the trend of a pant. Colored tops are not usually so much of a trend as opposed to how colored bottoms go in and out of style.

When something is a trend, be careful not to spend a lot of money on it. Spend money on staples, and items you will wear for a long time like coats, handbags, and shoes. If for example colored pants are a trend right now, don't buy the designer colored pants. Find an affordable version to wear so that when the trend passes, you won't feel like you spent a months paycheck on something that didn't last.

Instead, spend that hard earned money on timeless classic pieces that you can wear for much longer. A coat you can wear for more than one season is a great example, especially if its in a basic color such as the black, white, cream, or chocolate. The same comments that I mentioned about and tops can be applied to coats. Once the basics are covered, you can get a little more adventurous with your coats and start exploring different colors and textures.

Some of my favorites include cashmere, leather, suede, a brocade pattern, fur or faux fur. If you get colored coats, make sure they are made with quality fabric, otherwise it just looks cheap. For example, if a coat is a cotton candy pink color, it needs to be real leather or suede not pleather or any cheap fabric because the combination of a color and non quality fabric will make the whole thing look inexpensive. Alternatively, a fabric in a neutral color like black or camel brown is not as noticeable as a loud color in the same fabric.

My personal style code is that once I have basic items, I like to get colors in everything in all categories. I am a collector of fabric and style. I have every texture and color in my closet. So I apply this logic to all categories tops, bottoms, coats, accessories handbags and shoes. I have every color in the rainbow and then some from the turquoises to coral to lavender, color block, gold lace etc. The same goes for my coats. I have a beautiful dark purple brocade that gives me a Breakfast at Tiffanys, Jackie O type of vibe.

It is very ladylike and retro as well as classic. I love that the color is not a basic color - its purple so it gives it a little pop. I have a leather cotton candy pink trench coat that gives me a little pink panther/inspector gadget all wrapped in one since the coat is made with quality fabric, it doesn't look cheap. It just gives a pop to something that is classic, which is the trench coat, and adds a modern spin to it with the color.

The rule of thumb is that you should always focus on building off of what you have. Adding in an extra detail makes a plain outfit a standout. A plain tank top with jeans and an added scarf and some bangles, hoops in your ears, a platform or gladiator sandals or wedge shoes will take an outfit to another level. This is a good idea as opposed to having that same old tank top and jeans with no accessories no scarf and just some plain sandals. Just picture the difference between these two outfits.

Don't forget that details are important. You can add a blazer to that same look and you will look pulled together and polished. Almost every outfit can be 'dressed up". Its all about accessories, shoes, and a handbag that will determine the casualness or dressiness of a look.

HANDBAGS

"I'm thinking balls are to men, what purses are to women. It's just a little bag, but we'd feel naked in public without it."

— SARAH JESSICA PARKER AS CARRIE BRADSHAW

Handbags

Now that we have shoes out of the way, this leads me into discussing handbags; another trustworthy friend. Your purse goes with every weight and clothes size. Handbags are like shoes, and are another accessory to your overall look. They also can make your overall look seem that much more luxurious or quality. A nice handbag, even worn with something casual makes the whole ensemble look more expensive. Even if the outfit is not expensive, its about knowing how to mix high and low value items to always give the look of quality. Purses and shoes, even if not designer or name brand, can still be of quality, depending on whether the bag is made of leather.

A quality no name bag is better than a name brand bag of lesser quality fabric. If you want designer handbags and or shoes, there are places to get them at a better price than fresh off of the runway. There are always vintage shops, high end consignment shops and departments discount stores and or outlets like Nordstroms Off the Rack, Neimans Last Call and Saks Off the Fifth. These are the discount stores of those major department stores that have better price points.

Its important that everyone knows where to go to shop and buy clothing during the off season for best prices. This does not just apply to handbags but, everything in your wardrobe from clothes, coats, accessories, shoes, and purses. Now back to handbags, you need your basic colors, which are my first rule in every category we have talked about throughout this book. You need your classic black, white, brown and possibly a cream or blush color that is kind of a neutral color that is not too dark or too white.

Having bags in the primary colors should be where you
invest your dollars. You also want to make sure they are made of
quality fabrics. You want them to be timeless and classic so you can
always carry them.

So save any bags with fringe or over the top hardware or su- per trendy etc. for the other colors like purple, green, yellow orange, blue. I like bags in every color, so they go with most of your shoes and your clothes. Also bags of different shapes such as hobo, clutch, a messenger bag, or a big slouchy bag a briefcase style of bag. Mix up shapes and colors to coordinate with the variety of pieces that are in your wardrobe...

> **"Fashion is a language that creates itself in clothes to interpret reality."** Karl Lagerfeld

In conclusion, it is important to remember that everything you buy and wear should work together and these basic rules discussed in this book can be easily applied to make a fantastic wardrobe. I wanted to come up with a basic way to help women with style, women who don't have a Masters degree in Design from an accredited Fashion school. I wanted to provide a simple and fun way to reevaluate your look, wardrobe, and style and give it a little extra umph.

I wanted to do this without overwhelming people with a detailed lecture on fashion history or a major designer lecture on how to be stylish. I have included some quotes from the greats in this book, but didn't want to overwhelm someone who just wants to look good and would not recognize a Prada piece from a Gucci piece. It's not about the fashion and trends wearing you, but you conquering them to be the best you, and feeling good about how you present yourself to the world. I sincerely hope this book was fun and informative and helps you become a more stylish, put-together and fabulous you!

"The most important thing to remember is that you can wear all the greatest clothes and all the greatest shoes, but you've got to have a good spirit on the inside. That's what's really going to make you look like you're ready to rock the world."

— Alicia Keys

www.ingramcontent.com/pod-product-compliance
Lightning Source LLC
Chambersburg PA
CBHW042051290426
44110CB00001B/28